The F---

Bomb

UNEARTHING AND DISARMING ANXIETY LAND MINES IN EVERYDAY LIFE

Nahchon D. Guyton

The F--- Bomb. Copyright © 2020. Nahchon D. Guyton. All rights reserved.

No part of this book may be reproduced, stored in a retrieval system, or transmitted in any form or by any means, electronic, mechanical, photocopying, recording or otherwise, without prior permission of the author.

Published by:

ISBN: 978-1-949343-95-3 (paperback)

Scripture taken from the New King James Version®. Copyright © 1982 by Thomas Nelson. Used by permission. All rights reserved.

For more information on Nahchon D. Guyton, visit www.nahchon.com and feel free to leave your comments and opinions about this book and your personal journey.

Dedication

I dedicate this book to my Heavenly Father, who loved me first.

To my eldest Brother in the kingdom, Jesus the Christ, who suffered death in my place that I may have a chance to choose life.

To my Comforter, Counselor and Friend, the Holy Spirit, who guides, directs and teaches me His ways, so I can continue to grow and be transformed into a Son of the most high God who rules the Kingdom of Heaven.

Table of Contents

Dedication iii
To The Reader 7
Introduction 11
    Basic Solution 19
Chapter 1 21
Never Scarred But Fear The Walking Dead 21
Chapter 2 31
Don't Lie To Yourself, If You Don't Want To Be Lied To 31
    How To Detect Your Own Lies 32
    Examples of Self-Deception 35
    Lesson 1 - Seek Out Positive People 38
    Lesson 2 - First Be A Friend To Yourself 39
    Lesson 3 - Learn To Live In The Present And Release The Past 39
Chapter 3 43
Born Supernatural, But Living A Mundane Life 43

Lesson 4 - Enjoy The Moments By Journaling About Them 50

Lesson 5 - Have An Attitude Of Gratitude 51

Lesson 6 - Smile Yourself Happy 51

Chapter 4 53

Doing Life In The Face Of Fear 53

Chapter 5 59

Trusting The Love Of Christ For Us In The Face Of Our Crisis 59

Lesson 7 - Life Happens, But Do Not Expect The Worse 66

Lesson 8 - Develop An Attitude Of Thankfulness 66

Lesson 9 - Live Well By Understanding The Risk 66

Chapter 6 69

Know You Can, Even When The World Says You Can't 69

How To Move Past Fear 74

Use Your Words 77

Prayer 81

To The Reader

What is an F-Bomb? F-bomb in language is a dirty, foul curse word. The F-bomb I am talking about should be classified as a dirty word as well. I am speaking about FEAR, the most dangerous emotion in our lexicon of emotions. It is more dangerous than anger, guilt and shame rolled together. Anger, guilt, and shame often show up at events where fear attaches itself to its victims like a living parasite, then follows them everywhere, even into their dreams.

A close cousin to this feeling is "caution." This we must have to aid us in navigating dangerous terrains. We need caution in our life, not fear. When fear is fully grown, we become paralyzed. Being unable to move forward, we get stuck in a thought loop, a place of dread, anxiety, and insecurity. This is an F-Bomb: unchecked, un-faced fear that has exploded in our life and has become a pit of terror. It stops us from being who we were designed to be: courageous, victorious and an overcomer. Our world explodes from within and we are stopped from progressing, not able to move ahead; fear has exploded and left our dreams damaged, stifled and, in the worse cases, dead.

Questions come to mind: Why am I here? Why do I feel this way? What is wrong with me? We all came into the world with gifts, talents and skills that will not only benefit us but the world at large.

When we were created, God packed us with talents that would help us improve the world we are created to rule. We were not destined to rule each other but the world. What gifts do you possess that you have been suppressing just to fit in? No one comes to earth without gifts, purpose, or talents. However, most of us have been brainwashed into believing that we are nothing special or significant. We have been arrested by doubts, assaulted by insecurity, raped by anxiousness, and slain by fear.

When we were young, we were victims of the nuclear fallout of fear. Those F-Bombs were detonated in and around the lives, memories, and vicinity of the adults in our world. The youths are often victims by association, proximity, and genetics. Fear is passed down through the DNA like curly hair, brown eyes, and cleft chins. Are you walking around afraid of something but never encountered the thing you fear so greatly?

Ewen Callaway from Nature Magazine on December 1, 2013 wrote an article that has proven that fear can be passed down. Ewen explained that certain fears can be inherited through the generations based on a provocative study of mice reports. Some studies have hinted that environmental factors can influence biology more rapidly through "epigenetic" modifications, which alter the expression of genes, but not their actual nucleotide sequence.

Children who were conceived during a harsh wartime famine in the Netherlands in the 1940s are at increased risk of diabetes, heart disease and other conditions - possibly because of epigenetic alterations to genes involved in these diseases.

Kerry Ressler, a neurobiologist and psychiatrist at Emory University in Atlanta, Georgia, and a co-author of the latest study that was published in Nature Magazine, became interested in epigenetic inheritance after working with poor people living in inner cities, where cycles of drug addiction, neuropsychiatric illness and other problems often seem to recur in parents and their children.

Despite never having encountered acetophenone in their lives, the offspring exhibited increased sensitivity when introduced to its smell, shuddering more markedly in its presence compared with the descendants of mice that had been conditioned to be startled by a different smell or that had gone through no such conditioning.

In the fearful mice, the acetophenone-sensing gene of sperm cells had fewer methylation marks, which could have led to greater expression of the odorant-receptor gene during development. Humans inherit epigenetic alterations that influence behaviour, too, Ressler suspects. A parent's anxiety, he speculates, could influence later generations through epigenetic modifications to receptors for stress hormones.

It is all a part of the genes. Youths are born in fear and often raised in doubt, shame and riddled with guilt from the machine guns of fearful adults, who fear for the lives of the young like they did their own. Fear has killed not one, but several generations just by exploding in the life of one. Fear is a cancer that spreads like wildfire on the California hillsides. Often starting small in an unknown location, then before long it is out of control, destroying everything in its path. Fear can be passed down to our children. It must be stopped in us, if we do not want it to infect our children's children.

In this book you will discover how to stop fear and disarm the anxiety landmines that have covered the fields of our lives.

Introduction

> I will praise thee; for I am fearfully and wonderfully made: marvelous are thy works; and that my soul knoweth right well. (Psalm 139:14 – KJV)

Fearfully here does not mean full of fear; it means made in a manner to impress admiration and astonishment.

The truth is, when God created us, He made us good and without the spirit of fear. We are not what we have been told. We are what we say and, more importantly, what God says. We were created with a design that only the Father knows. He allows us to enhance the design by the words of our mouth. For this reason, the enemy works hard to keep us confused about who we are and what we can do, if we live and act in faith. The devil knows that we have all power that was in Christ Jesus. Therefore, instead of us building a relationship with Jesus and Father God, he would have us build a dependency on religion and culture. In other words, we have been fed a diet of "FAKE NEWS," a counterfeit to the "Good News" of the Kingdom. By so doing, we think we are going somewhere but we are like a dog chasing its tale: all movement with no progress. We are just in motion going nowhere; a circle of despair, doubt, fear, shame - repeat. This cycle goes on and on until we are violently interrupted. This book is all about that violent interruption that will get you to stop the devastation and the spread of the F-Bomb fallout.

God created us, but the spirit of fear was not a part of the original design. He created us to rule, to dominate, to be fruitful (productive), to multiply and to create something more than what we see. The devil knows that you are more powerful than you could ever perceive, even by yourself. He knows that he is no match for you, if you are faith-built and fearless. He keeps you isolated so he can put you on a slow drip of fear, doubt, shame, and anxiety. He feeds you these negative emotions intravenously, knowing that what is inside will come out. This is how the virus of fear spreads. It spreads through the people, the living hosts, who can be likened to confused zombies resembling the "Walking Dead" and not the source code of God the Almighty.

Satan, also known as the devil, knows that you are powerful and have been endowed with dominion, courage, and faith by our Father God. You were created with love, power, and a sound mind. The enemy uses your creative right to destroy you. What do I mean? He knows that you have the power to create worlds with your words, so he messes with your situation to get you to say something in fear. What is a fear statement? It is a statement that you say about what you do not want. You repeat the chaos your senses perceive, giving them life with your tongue, hung by the very thing you feared. You saw, you spoke it, agreed with it and now it is alive and destroying you. The issue with this is that your power is one direction; it will only produce the thing you dread, instead of producing the desires of your faith-filled heart. When you speak in fear, you produce what you said you did not want. The enemy knows that he does not have to hurt you but set a trap and allow your fear to destroy you.

How does this work? The enemy is you. The devil has power, rule, and subjects but he and all his subjects are not more powerful than you. Yes, you are more powerful than the devil, if you are in Christ Jesus. All power in heaven and hell belongs to Jesus and he left it with you. So yes, if you are in Jesus you have the right and authority to cast out all darkness, including fear, in and through the name of Jesus Christ.

How do you cast out fear? You must move in faith, speak in faith, and walk by faith. Living in faith is the only way to cast out fear. Faith is our key to disarming all the F-Bombs and anxiety land mines in our life.

THE F--- BOMB

Anxiety can be described as any or a combination of feelings that all have their roots in some type of fear, including unease, worry, apprehension, dread, powerlessness, or a sense of impending danger – real or imagined. Symptoms can be wide-ranging: the mind goes blank or other cognitive functions are lost, obsessive thoughts, phobias, chronic worry, ongoing unease, sweaty palms, tension headaches, trembling, difficulty breathing, dizziness, panic attacks, increased heart rate and palpitations.

"Worry is a thin stream of fear trickling through the mind. If encouraged, it cuts a channel into which all other thoughts are drained."

~ Arthur Somers Roche, American journalist, writer, 1883-1935.

According to the National Institute of Mental Health, forty (40) million American adults – that is eighteen percent (18%) of the population – have anxiety disorders, which often begin in childhood.

Social phobia alone: when people become overwhelmingly anxious and excessively self-conscious in everyday social situations, affects fifteen (15) million adults, and specific phobias: an intense fear of something that poses little or no actual danger, affects nineteen point two (19.2) million adults in the U.S.

It is the goal of this book to help persons who are suffering with anxiety, depression, fear, and anger issues. These persons will learn how to disarm the F-bombs in their lives and dig-up the anxiety and anger land mines they have set in place as protection from hurt, pain and discomfort. It is not uncommon for someone with an anxiety disorder to also suffer from depression, anger or some other phobia that prevents them from living a full life. Nearly one-half of those diagnosed with depression are also diagnosed with an anxiety disorder. Over three (3) million American citizens suffer with some form of Anxiety each year. In truth, these land mines have become the very thing that has kept them isolated and a stranger to the people closest to them. When someone feels alone or unknown, they often fall into the pits of depression. What they do not realize is that the pit has been dug by their own hands.

A land mine, as defined by the Merriam-Webster Dictionary, is "a mine usually placed just below the surface of the ground and designed to be exploded usually by the weight of vehicles or troops passing over it —often used figuratively."[1]

Read that definition once more aloud; it is an explosive placed just below the surface of the ground designed to be activated when the weight of something passes over it. This is what an anxiety land mine is: a fear that explodes in your life when the pressures of life move over an issue that you buried just below the surface. This is where in America we get the saying, "walking on eggshells." What it means is that the slightest thing can set a person off.

As you read through the F-bomb, it is my goal that you learn to recognize and dig up the anxiety land mines that you buried just beneath the surface. In an effort to create a barrier of protection for yourself, you have built a volatile and explosive environment based on a hidden or unrecognized fear that is now controlling your every move and the moves of the people around you. You have barricaded yourself, trying to protect yourself. You are fear-controlled, not love-exposed. Love will and cancels all fears, but love requires exposure. It needs to shine its light; light shines brightest in the dark.[2]

---

[1] https://www.merriam-webster.com/dictionary/land%20mine
[2] According to ADAA.org Facts and Statistics page. https://adaa.org/about-adaa/press-room/facts-statistics searched on September 28, 2019

I am not a doctor or a therapist. Even though I am a certified Life Coach, the information in this book is to help individuals handle the cause of both anxiety and depression from a natural and spiritual perspective. I am not an advocate for medication, in most cases, but for some it is essential. If that is you, then do what you need to do to manage your issues. As for the others, keep reading and let us unpack, disarm, and eliminate the F-Bombs in our daily lives.

Thomas was a normal sixteen-year-old boy, until he was in a bad car accident that almost killed him. Thomas was leaving basketball practice and on his way home. Upon reaching a four-way intersection, he stopped and out of nowhere, something ran into him from behind and hit the passenger side. The impact was so great that the car Thomas was in was nearly crushed. Thomas had to be air lifted to the nearest hospital. He was in surgery for sixteen hours due to swelling on his brain. Thomas survived and recovered, but not fully. Every time he approaches a four-way intersection, he has anxiety and begins to panic. The doctors prescribed some anti-depression medication for him, but he stopped taking them because they made him angry and suicidal at times.

This story is true, but Thomas is a composite of many people who have fallen victim to fear and the dark weight of accidents that hit us all, at some point in life. Similarly, many people have anxiety after a major life-altering event. They never quite get over or through the trauma that befell them. Now they are in an anxiety and fear loop. This loop is destroying them little by little, day by day. When they get upset or frustrated, the words they say to themselves can trigger greater feelings of anxiety, which reactivates the anxiety, fear, and depression loop.

While there are new "problems" surfacing all the time, many are extensions of old familiar problems or, at the least, existing problems that we already know how to resolve. That is why some people spend their lives finding patterns in solutions. We all have problems in our lives. There are numerous problems in our local and national governments. I would recommend that you focus on disarming at least one fear land mine in your personal life, but it is your choice, right? One thing that makes diffusing f-bombs and anxiety land mines in our lives difficult is that not everyone sees something as a problem. If you do not see it as a problem but everyone around you does, you will not make any effort to resolve the issue because you do not see the problem for what it is. It is a land mine just waiting to go off in your life. Think about what is more important: your way or a better way? Most F-bombs are ignited from a past event that we have not dealt with. We suppressed the fear instead of confronting it with open eyes and hearts in order to resolve the issue. Now imagine doing this repeatedly. At some point suppressing will create discomfort and the space to suppress will no longer be available. Now you are a walking time bomb looking for a place to go off.

Basic Solution

Cause: They tend to use a lot of negative words when thinking about themselves.

Basic Solution: Learning to refocus their internal dialogue and feelings when they start down this land mine laden path is helpful.

This book is written for those persons who want to find another way to deal with trauma other than medication. This book is for those persons who want to live an abundant life and not one laced with anxiety, angry outburst and wakes of destruction that seem to follow them. This book is for that person who knows there is more to life than what he or she is living up to this point. Last but not least, this book is for the small wounded child in all of us who is crying out, screaming loudly but no one seems to hear. Fear has taken hold and has bounded this child. For that inner child who may have grown up in age, but still lives from and rarely steps out of that cage where fear first arrested and took him or her hostage, this is for you. If you are that person, keep reading and let us remove

THE F--- BOMB

these F-bombs from our lives together. To be clear, we are not immune to F-bombs popping up in our lives, but we can disarm them, if we are willing to face them together.

Chapter 1
Never Scarred But Fear The Walking Dead

You are shopping for groceries or buckling your seat belt when suddenly your muscles contract and your heart begins to pound. Panic attacks can be both bewildering and terrifying, but they are not unusual. Many sufferers believe they are having a heart attack and rush to the emergency room. This was the case with a friend of mine named Juan. We were sitting at lunch, laughing, and talking as we often did, when suddenly Juan grabbed his chest, started to sweat, and could hardly speak. We called 911, "I think my friend is having a heart attack!" I said. The ambulance arrived quickly, and Juan was rushed off to the hospital.

My co-workers and I waited with great anticipation to hear what was happening. Juan was not even thirty years old so there was no reason he should be having a heart attack. Hours seemed like days and still no word on what was happening and if Juan was dead or alive. I did not know everyone was looking at me for answers since Juan and I would often hang out after work. I was just as bewildered as they were. I called Juan's wife, no answer. I was puzzled, confused and afraid for the fate of my friend. The next day, at around 10:00 a.m., Juan appeared with a smile on his face and looked healthier than ever. "Dude, what happened man? We thought you were dying?" I exclaimed.

Juan smiled and said, "No, they told me I just had a panic attack."

"A panic attack? How?" I asked with childlike curiosity. He said that was the diagnosis. "Have you ever had one of those before?" I questioned.

Juan answered, "Yeah, I use to get gripped with fear and couldn't move for several minutes. Those minutes felt like hours. I only got them after I watched a thriller or scary movie. I have had nothing like that since I was twelve or maybe thirteen."

So, I asked, "Did you watch a scary movie last night?"

He laughed and said, "Man, no. I was with you watching the Matrix."

I said, "Yeah, you're right. Maybe you were afraid of Neo, no Mr. Smith?"

He smiled and said, "No I wasn't. You know how many times I have watched that movie?"

I said, "The fact that you can quote most of the lines by heart, I would say a hell of a lot." We laughed and continued to discuss some work matters.

Later that day, I asked some of our co-workers if they had ever experienced a panic attack. Most said no but one person said yes. He explained that he had one when he was a teen but nothing since then. I used to have panic attacks when I was a child, but I never really understood what was happening. I suffered from asthma so I would often confuse the panic attack with my asthma. It was not until years later I found out that I was having a panic attack. It came often out of the blue and left just as it came.

The cause of an attack can be unclear, but they often arise in the face of major life changes, such as childbirth or a new job.

What is a panic attack? It is more than a feeling of anxiety; a panic attack produces distinctive physical symptoms. Each person experiences panic differently, but most people report intense fear accompanied by bodily sensations that can range from a racing heart to nausea and dizziness.

This is an example of an F-Bomb going off.

THE F--- BOMB

The "Walking Dead" is a very popular American television show that depicts a not so distant future where there is a bio-chemical outbreak and people become zombies after they die. The picture they paint is a world where every day is a matter of life or death. The people that are not infected are not to be trusted and resources are limited as the zombies have overrun the world. You must move in stealth, as loud noise attracts the zombies and causes them to attack. To defeat the zombies, you must take off their heads. No matter how many times you shoot them in the body, they will continue to move toward you with the goal of turning you into a zombie. They want to bite you, eat you and this is how you get infected. Once you are infected, you become a part of them when you die, so the infected band together to hunt the uninfected. This is how the F-bombs work in our daily lives. Once one goes off, we infect the people around us, then they, in turn, do the same thing repeatedly. Once persons have been exposed to an F-bomb, they are now like the walking dead. They become afraid to live life to the fullest, not knowing who they can trust or if their current supply will be enough. They hoard, rob and steal and, in the worst cases, they kill. They aim to take out as many non-infected persons as possible before they destroy themselves. Why? What makes a seemingly normal person grow so cold, so distant, and so cruel to another? This is what we want to explore: the why behind the F-Bombs.

In today's fast-paced world, we are more stressed, more tired, and, in spite of all the ways to connect, we are more disconnected from others. We have our government fighting from within and our enemies threatening to go to war. Mass school shootings have become more common; the economy is often in a flux, so we feel anxious about what is next; where do we turn for surety. How can we be safe? How can we live in peace? How can we survive the mental invasion of the next catastrophic event? What ill-fate will befall us next? Infectious diseases are floating through the air, like honing missiles set to destroy its target quickly, with little external damage, except to spread to the next none-expecting victim. One virus has been a highly effective killing machine and is extremely contagious: the flu. The flu exterminates an average of fifteen thousand persons yearly. Fear is like the flu; it comes in on the silence of the air and consumes all that is in its sphere, infecting many and using others as carriers of its deadly mission: to destroy the hope of all it touches and to eliminate faith and all desire of recovery. Fear feeds on doubt like cancer feeds on sugar, and can spread like a wildfire, from victim to victim; all it takes is a drop of fear to spread death to countless victims. It lives to inflict misery on many, not fast or quick, but slow, deliberate, rhythmic - like a slow methodic drip of an IV connected to the soul of faith in the heart of humanity. Who are our friends and where are our enemies? Do my family and friends really love me? If so, why do they treat me this way? Why don't I have any true friends? Do some or all these questions sound familiar? They should, if you have ever been the victim of an F-bomb.

The "F" word I am speaking of does not rhyme with duck, but year. The "F" bomb I am speaking of is fear. Fear is just that: a bomb. It will blow your world up and leave more devastation than you know. You stayed in that dead-end job because you were afraid to move to a better opportunity and walk in your gift. You stayed in that destructive relationship because you were afraid of what? Being alone, hurting their feelings or whatever lie you told yourself at the time the fear bomb exploded and kept you from being your best. You have become infected, and the infection is highly contagious. If you do not disarm those F-bombs, you too will become a carrier of this deadly infection known as fear.

Fear is subtle; it creeps in on the wings of caution and makes camp. It draws lines in the sand that say things like, "I will never let this, that or the other happen to me ever again. I refuse to forget or forgive." Fear builds walls in your life. It keeps you from moving beyond your limited knowledge to interact with someone who looks, sounds, and thinks differently from you. Fear holds you and your potential captive. Fear will not allow you to move from what is comfortable to the unknown. Caution is not like fear; it does not set up camp. Caution is like a lazy river, it moves, but slowly and deliberately. It is watching, searching, and looking forward as it moves. It is okay to be cautious but never fearful. Fear will and can blow your world up. You are where you are because you are held captive by fear.

I can now hear you saying, "That is not true. I didn't do this because of…" You can run me a whole line of, "why nots" and "how comes" but the truth of the matter is, you are stuck and paralyzed by your fear. Oh, my apologies, I forgot to tell you that even though fear is universal, it is also personal. Your fear is what keeps you from achieving, reaching, building, and sharing your gifts with the world. Just like my fear kept me from being my best. That is why I am telling you this; I have overcome my fear, pushed past the campsite of comfortable and moved into the rush of what could be. I feel fear every day, every moment of the day. I press forward with caution and leave fear where it is, a "False Event Appearing Real." I honestly do not know what tomorrow or the next second will bring but I do know that from here, and until I get there, I will not be held captive by an illusion any longer. There is an American saying that goes like this, "If you're not a part of the solution, then you are a part of the problem." This saying was penned by Eldredge Cleaver.

THE F--- BOMB

This quote and varieties of it appear to be credited to one or two individuals, including an African, but the longer form goes as follows:

> "There is no more neutrality within the world. You either have to be part of the solution, or you're going to be part of the problem."

This is one of those duality quotes where you are instantly tossed into one of two camps: the solution camp or the issue camp. This quote forces you to ask yourself, what camp will you rest yourself: solution or issue? When it comes to F-bombs, you have to pick a camp; you are either disarming them or you are helping to plant them. There are no two ways about it. You say, "Nahchon, how can you say that? You don't know me or what I have been through. How dare you tell me about me?" I am not telling you about you, per se, I am telling you about human nature; the natural unchecked flow of people when it comes to F-bombs or fear. People either fan it to a full-blown explosion or quench it with the cool headedness of courage. There is no middle ground here. Let me ask you this question, "Can you sit on the sidelines and not be part of the issue, if you make conscious choices not to make a difference?" I have my take on this question. However, it is not for me to answer, but rather you.

What is your stance on F-bombs: are you for or are you against them? Think about it, and you will understand why as you read on.

Chapter 2
Don't Lie To Yourself, If You Don't Want To Be Lied To

> I love those who can smile in trouble, who can gather strength from distress, and grow brave by reflection. 'Tis the business of little minds to shrink, but they, whose heart is firm and whose conscience approves their conduct, will pursue their principles unto death.
>
> ~ Leonardo da Vinci

We fool ourselves into believing things that are false—and—we refuse to believe things that are true.[3] In fact, we lie to ourselves about everything, from why we like wearing designer clothing instead of no-name brand fashion, to

---

[3] TEDx Honest Liars: The Psychology of Self-Deception

how our childhood influenced our choice of romantic partners.

Given the unconscious nature of self-deception, becoming honest presents us with a serious dilemma: How do we know when we are lying to ourselves? Clearly, you cannot directly ask yourself if you are lying because that would require you to tell the truth. The most important way to determine whether you are lying or not is to observe yourself, without judgment or evaluation.

How To Detect Your Own Lies

Notice Your Emotions

For example, if you struggle with trust issues in your romantic relationships, you may feel anxious, angry, or scared when falling in love with a new mate. In fact, your reaction is fundamentally based on who you are and unresolved issues from your past that you are bringing into your new relationship. Given this reality, when you have a strong emotional reaction to something or someone, pause. Ask yourself, "Is my emotions really related to the present situation or is the present situation triggering something in me that is unresolved baggage from my past?"

Notice Your Thoughts

In fact, most of us believe that we are right about everything: we think our thoughts are true. These thoughts can be very negative, such as, "I am sure my new partner is cheating on me because my ex cheated" or "I am scared to fall in love because I am going to get hurt." Or they can be overly positive, like, "This is the most amazing person in the world." Given this reality, when you notice your thinking is extreme or irrational, pause.

Notice Your Behavior

We desperately want our behavior to be separate from our identity. For example, you do not want to admit that you are jealous, even though you check your partners' phone messages more than normal. The truth is that our behavior reflects who we are in some way. When your behavior is inconsistent with whom you want or claim to be, pause. Ask yourself, "What is motivating my behavior? What do I not want to admit to myself about my behavior?"

We cannot be honest with others, until we are first honest with ourselves. By observing our emotions, thoughts, and behaviors, we can learn about who we really are and give ourselves the opportunity to change. You may be asking yourself, "Why should I care about self-deception? What is the benefit to me?" Although normal and common place in our society, self-deception comes with profound costs because we live our truth, whether we are honest about it or not. Anytime our lives are driven by something outside of our awareness, it is dangerous to us and everyone around us. One major cost of self-deception is that we hurt ourselves and those we love the most when we do not take full responsibility for who we are. One of the hardest people to be completely honest with is yourself. It is so much easier to fool you and remain ignorant, than to own up to what is real. Fooling yourself is easy to do and is the preferred option for most people. Lying to you is essentially living in denial and a world of falseness, sad to say this is what a number of persons choose.

Another primary cost of self-deception is that we can contribute to large-scale acts of cruelty by believing our lies and spreading them to others. Although most of us deny that we are capable of deliberately harming others, history and a great deal of social psychology research suggest that we are all capable of extreme acts of cruelty when put in the right environment. People can lie to themselves in many ways. When people are having a difficult time reaching their goal, they sometimes convince themselves that the goal is not realistic and not worth following. This type of lie makes it easier to quit because you convince yourself that no amount of effort or persistence would have paid off in the end. This is not true. The thing about lying to yourself is that you get so deep into the lie that you no longer believe it to be a lie. At this point it is crucial that you work on creating a new trend of thought once you start down the path of denial.

Another major cost of self-deception is that it can leave us with massive amounts of regret. Looking back at life, regret is one of the hardest things to get over because you cannot change your choices in the past, only your choices in the present. If you are lying to yourself, you must ask why? The only way you can stop lying to yourself is if you are finally ready to admit the truth. This normally does not happen until you are confronted by the truth or forced to deal with reality in some way. Most lie to themselves in order to create the illusion of control, security or to feel okay. Self-deception is a branch on the tree of fear. It will grow and spread its leaves before you realize you are using your self-deception as a shade. You will begin to rest under it, instead of boldly confronting it with truth. Life is too long to live with regret and too short to live with fear. Make a choice to tell the truth, if to no one else but yourself.

Examples of Self-Deception

Example 1: A woman gets a high-paying attorney job at a popular firm. Convinced that she is just going through a bout of bad health, she continues working in her high-stress job until she has a nervous breakdown.

Example 2: A man is in a relationship with a lady who he accepts as his soulmate. The man proceeds to accept that the lady cherishes him, even after she has repeatedly told him that she wants to break up.

Example 3: A student is planning for a college exam. He finds himself, as often as possible, delaying and saying that he is not in the mood to study. He, at that point, takes the exam and comes up short.

Example 4: A lady has joined a nearby church. She adores hearing sermons about love, acceptance, and kindness. She turns a "blind eye" on the cutthroat behavior of some individuals, persuading herself that she is on the "right ethical path."

Lies are little fortresses; inside them you can feel safe and powerful. Through your little fortress of lies you try to run your life and manipulate others.

The fortress, however, needs walls, so you can build some. These are the justifications for your lies. You know, like you are doing this to protect someone you love, to keep them from feeling pain. Whatever works, just so you feel okay about the lies.

> There are several things in the world that can kill us, but nothing like fear.

~ William Paul Young

Psychology 101 educates students all over that other than food, water, and air, the most essential of human needs is security. News and media outlets build their gathering of people i.e. viewers by sensationalizing genuine and/or perceived dangers to their viewers' individual and outside security. We are effortlessly captivated by the stun and frightfulness of common calamities and man's persistent capability to commit intolerable acts (like fear mongering or recordings of decapitating, etc.).

If we are to be honest with ourselves, we would have to admit that we are where we are because of our fears. I know things happen, sometimes really bad things that set you back. That is just it, a setback, it is not permanent and because of fear we make permanent decisions based on temporary situations. That makes just as much sense as building a house on the ocean during low tide. At some point in time the tide will rise, now look, your house has been washed away. This is what life is; it is low and high tides. Fear is always working to keep you stuck, so you let your hopes, dreams, and skills wither on the vine of possibility, because you were infected with fear.

THE F--- BOMB

Fear is real, it is as real as you let it be. Yes, the feelings come but that is not what stops you; it is when you believe the feeling over what is true.

Headlines can and often infect us with fear. Some people are frightened by the idea of rejection or disapproval and, still, others fear disasters of some sort.

What do you do with the barrage of threats that hit you every day? How can you create a sense of peace and live in an optimistic way, when you are bombarded by fears from both the outside and inside? You are always with you, nowhere to run; no place to hide. You are forever present with you. Here are our first lessons in disarming the F-bombs in our lives.

Lesson 1 - Seek Out Positive People

Let their joy and happiness feed you and let their energy of good vibration resonate in your soul. Allow their positive attitudes to take you to a higher altitude. Studies have proven that we feel happier around happy people. Find those people in your life. If no one can be found close to you, seek them out. It is crucial to your thriving-ability that you learn how to encourage yourself through experiences and develop the positive state of mind you crave. Once you have tasted the positive output from those persons, replay the positive messages you have heard from those you love and respect. Then, to make the lesson stick, be that to yourself and others.

Lesson 2 - First Be A Friend To Yourself

When you hear the voice of fear, self-doubt, or criticism in your head, write yourself a letter of encouragement. Write an email of congratulation for being courageous today and set it to send to yourself three days from today.

Lesson 3 - Learn To Live In The Present And Release The Past

Take a time-out to redirect your thoughts to the present moment. Focus on your breath and how it feels filling your lungs and belly, then leaving your body through a slow exhale. Notice any tension in your body as you breathe? Five minutes each day can help you feel more at peace and less stressed out. If you are a person of faith, find a place to pray. Let your imagination allow you to know that our heavenly Father cares for you and is there in your life. Let your fears be lifted by the power of a loving God. Breathe deeply and let your Creator touch your heart.

> America was not built on fear. America was built on courage, on imagination and

> an unbeatable determination to do the job at hand.
>
> ~ Harry S. Truman

Do not be stuck like I was; do not allow another moment to pass where you are held hostage by fear, enslaved by fear and refuse to move forward because it feels so real. We have so many sayings about unsure situations like, "Keep your feet planted firmly on the ground." I am sorry but that is fear speaking. Yes, you should move with caution, jump with caution but do not stay grounded with it. When you refuse to move, that is no longer caution but fear at work. The next time you feel stuck, ask yourself, "What am I afraid of?" Deal with it and move forward. There is too much life to live to be stuck where you are until next time. Be your best; you are the only one who can do it for you.

> Action is a great restorer and builder of confidence. Inaction is not only the result, but the cause of fear. Perhaps the action you take will be successful; perhaps different action or adjustments will have

to follow. But any action is better than no action at all.

~ Norman Vincent Peale

Fear is a construct of the flesh operating in the mind. Your mind does not know the difference between dreams and reality. It does not recognize or compute the words cannot, should not or do not. No matter how much you don't want something, the more you talk and think about what you don't want, the more you will get the very thing. Your mind does not compute those words. To deal with fear effectively is to use the power of words, to talk, think and meditate on what you want. This is how you feed the subconscious. When you focus on what you do not want, you often end up getting just that. Fear works like faith, just in reverse. When you hope for a better future and work towards it, you get better. The same is true when you worry about the future and all the things that can go wrong or will go wrong; your fear manifests into your reality. Fear is a mental image of the worse and faith is a mental image of the best. Now some would say they are just being realistic; I say you are being weak-minded and fear-driven. You have tapped into your superpower of imagination but misplaced it. A hero is only one intentional act away from being a villain. Fear is the ultimate villain; it steals moments of your life, days of opportunity, weeks of rest, and years of joy. Yes, fear is the deadliest of F-bombs one could ever hope to encounter anywhere on the planet.

There are several things in the world that can kill us, but nothing like fear, anxiety, and depression; the three horsemen of the "Hope-Apocalypse." They are riding around the earth looking for their next victim; do not be that victim. Fight for your dreams, hold fast to your hope and turn from fear. Do not run but tap into your superpower and crush fear with hope, faith, and determination. You were born supernatural, but we often settle for mediocrity.

Chapter 3
Born Supernatural, But Living A Mundane Life

> You gain strength, courage, and confidence by every experience in which you really stop to look fear in the face. You are able to say to yourself, "I lived through this horror. I can take the next thing that comes along."
>
> ~ Eleanor Roosevelt

We are all born with a superpower: it lies in how we choose to use it. Our imagination is the center for where our superpower is activated. We all have the power to create something. Some use their superpower to make music, art, poetry, and scientific discoveries, while others use it to destroy themselves and others. Drugs to get high, sex trafficking, drug trafficking, how to steal, rob and get over on their fellow man at the end of the day, all starts with the superpower of the imagination. This superpower becomes a WMD (Weapon of Mass Destruction) in our lives when we allow fear to infect it with dread, hopelessness, and anxiety of: What if it goes wrong? What if it goes right? Is it the best opportunity at this stage of your life? How would you know if you never move from where you think you are safe, to a place of courage? What would your life look like, if you stopped telling lies to yourself?

Fear is kryptonite to that superpower, as faith is vibranium. It will bring you into all manner of possibilities of what could be and allow you to go further than most could have dreamed. We all have superpowers; most of us are untrained in how to use them, so we think we do not have them. We have the power to create, we were created in the image and likeness of our Father in heaven. We have dominion, power, and authority over the whole earth. Therefore, we can say to this or that and it must obey us, if we do it in faith and doubt not. The issue is, we let the thing that we were created to dominate, dominate us. We are being dominated by paper that we made. The paper I am speaking of is money. We are being dominated by drink that we created. We have let our creation rule us, instead of us ruling it. How absurd is that? We have let our creation run us, instead of the other way around. Why have we done this? Because we have lied to ourselves and continue to lie and say we have no control over it. We invented it, so since we created it with our imagination, we must destroy it with our imagination.

I believe that the imagination is stronger than knowledge; that myth is more potent than history; that dreams are more powerful than facts; that hope always triumphs over experience; that laughter is the only cure for grief; that love is stronger than death.[4]

The F-bomb is wreaking havoc in our lives every day. We are self-destructing, not from the outside in, but from the inside out. We are destroying ourselves because of fear. Fear will kill your hope, steal your peace, and destroy your future. We must eliminate fear wherever we find it in ourselves. Fear has kept us from traveling to a foreign place that we longed to visit for years. It has stopped us from starting that business that we dreamed of for several years. It has destroyed our hope in people because we are afraid of the unknown. Fear is the greatest enemy of mankind in the world. Violence, climate change and global warming are not the things that will destroy mankind and the earth. Mankind and the earth will be eliminated by one thing and that is fear. Fear is the greatest threat to our survival than anything else on this planet. Yes, global warming is a

---

[4]Robert Fulghum

threat; yes, violence is damaging, and racial tension is also destructive. However, none of these can be compared to fear. Fear is why all these things are happening. Fear is the seed and the root, the rest are just symptoms of the disease of fear, not the cause. Fear is the cause.

Come go with me on a journey; let us travel to the early 1600's, when men were traveling the earth, discovering new lands, people and culture. When some people found new people, they embraced them, learned, and traded with them, while others feared them and came back to destroy those people and those lands. Some would say for power and control, others would say for expansion of said civilization. I say it was pure fear that drove people to war with others who did not attacked them first. A bully picks on people out of fear, not out of being superior. You do not bully whom you do not fear; you work with them. When you find someone threatening to your perspective, position, or views, you seek to destroy them. That is human nature, right? No, that is fallen human nature. We were created to work together, not against one another.

Fear separates, paralyzes, and destroys opportunities to grow. When we face fear head on, we learn that the fear was all in our minds and the actual event was less traumatic than you feared. The thing about fear is that it is really faith perverted. We make up in our minds and believe with our minds that the fear is real, so we do not move but become stained and frozen into a false sense of security that we are okay, when in reality we are a walking corpse who have died in the face of fear so many times. At this point the thought of doing something uncomfortable is enough to stop us dead in our tracks. Fear is similar to how they would train Elephants in the Circus. When the elephant is small, they chain them at the ankle with a large heavy chain and drive a stake far into the ground. No matter how hard the baby elephant tries, it cannot escape the grasp of the chain. As the elephant grows, it tries and tries till one day it gives up. It has been dominated, not by men with brute strength but by the imagination of man. Innovation and creativity are what dominated the elephant. Once the elephant has been dominated, all it takes is a small rope to stop the elephant from escaping. Once the elephant feels the resistance of the measly rope, the elephant gives up the fight. That small rope is fear. The mere tension of the rope stops the powerful full-grown elephant. Many studies say that elephants have the longest of memories. The elephant remembers that no matter how hard they try, they could not break free. This is the same for us; our memory of a past hurt, disappointment or failure is our rope that holds us captive. Know this, you are a full-grown conqueror, so push pass the false event appearing real; move pass your fear with determination.

THE F--- BOMB

This is no way to live, but many people fall victim to fear daily. The only way out is up; get up from your fear by moving in courage. It is not easy when you have convinced yourself that the fear is real. When your fear has built a house of lies, that you are not able to shake, the foundation is an illusion. All you must do is look at the fear and move past it. Most will feel the fear so strongly, thinking it is real. Their bodies then begin to betray them when they even think of what scares them. The feeling is so loud that logic is drowned out; the mind goes blank with nothing firing but fight or flight. Common sense is smothered, and hope is choked. Fear has won again.

To defeat fear is to face fear head-on with courage; facing fear while being afraid so you can realize that the darkness is not true darkness but a shadow that was cast by fear. Once you face your fear, it is like lifting the shade to let in the true light of hope. The shadows of fear instantly fade when we face fear. Do you feel scared when you do what you have never done? Yes, but you will feel empowered when you push pass that illusion of limitations and embrace the possibility of adventure, hope, and new horizons. You will better know that you have deconstructed the F_ _ _ bomb in your life, so it was not able to go off. You preserved not only your life but all those who witness you standing up to your fear, which is just a challenge. There is nothing in this world that we should fear. There are challenges of growth that we must take to go beyond where we are, to the place that God created for us to be. When does it all go bad? When we say that it is bad. I have a saying that I never lose; I either win or I learn, but I never lose. Since I have adopted this state-of-mind, when the three horsemen of the "hope-apocalypse" come running, looking to infect me, I am insulated, not isolated. I have a shield of faith, a wall of hope and a bunker of refuge to protect me. I rest in knowing that no matter what happens, I will learn something of great value that our heavenly Father will use to work it all out for my good. He will do the same for you, if you allow Him. First things first, we must disarm these F-bombs that keep popping up all over our everyday lives. Here are the next lessons in disarming the F-bombs of life.

Nowhere in the Bible will you find where fear was rewarded, only faith. Fear is you looking at what you can or cannot do without God. Faith is you trusting God with all of you, knowing that He has and will make everything work out to your good, if you trust Him. Do you want to live an abundant life, or a life stifled by fear? A life stifled by fear is a small life; selfish and non-productive. No one grows or is inspired when one fails to do what he or she was created to do. You were made to conquer, to have dominion over all the earth. Why live beneath your right?

Why submit to the world? You were created to rule over it, with God as your head and Jesus as the source of your strength. Do you really want to let another F-bomb go off in your life unchecked? If you answered, "Yes, I want to live a life of fear. I enjoy being a coward and being afraid of any and everything new and different. This is a life that is full for me; I know what to expect." I would say to you: You are delusional, and your fear has turned into complacency. You are not living but dying standing on your feet. Your life has left because you have no hope. Instead of living life, you are waiting to die. Where is your sense of hope? Where is your joy and search for something more? Life does not reward the fearful but only the courageous; the one who is willing to do it afraid.

Stay positive and happy. Work hard and do not give up hope. Be open to criticism and keep learning. Surround yourself with happy, warm, and genuine people.[5]

Lesson 4 - Enjoy The Moments By Journaling About Them

This can change your brain structure in positive ways. Writing about cherished memories and ideas strengthens the neurological pathways responsible for positive thought processes. Our brains naturally attend to negative aspects of

---

[5]Tena Desae

our environment to keep us safe. Retrain your brain to notice the joyful, empowering ones more easily.

Lesson 5 - Have An Attitude Of Gratitude

Appreciate the people, places, and activities that feed your soul. It is a normal part of life. That is what makes it so important to demonstrate gratitude and nurture the sources of your well-being at every opportunity.

Lesson 6 - Smile Yourself Happy

The act of smiling forces a chain reaction of muscular, hormonal, and neural activity that is associated with happiness. Laughter is associated with strengthening the immune system due to the physiology involved. Like medicine, laughter does the body good.

A merry heart doeth good like a medicine: but a broken spirit drieth the bones. (Proverbs 17:22 – KJV).

Chapter 4
Doing Life In The Face Of Fear

You gain strength, courage, and confidence from every experience in which you really stop to look fear in the face. You are able to say to yourself, "I lived through this horror. I can take the next thing that comes along."[6]

Stop thinking about what you cannot do. Instead, focus on what you can do. Refuse to give your doubts a second thought; cast them out immediately and place them at the foot of the cross. I know you are asking, "How do I do it? I am so afraid of failing." Let me help you with that. You are not going to fail. I told you how to do it, now you know what to expect. So, what is your excuse now? When you fail, it is going to hurt a little and you will not want to do it again but resist that notion and do it again. The only path to greatness is to be good. To be good, you will first have to be bad, and to be bad, it is you who must do it. Do it

---

[6]Eleanor Roosevelt

until you are at least good. Then, if you want to stop, let it be by choice and not because you are afraid.

I was seven years old when I learned that I was deafly afraid of water. I heard so many stories of people drowning. My father almost drowned and I remember going to the location where he almost drowned when I was five years old; he pointed it out to me. I do not remember him saying, "Be afraid of water," but the story of him almost drowning did something to me. I did not want to be in water, if it came over my waist. I loved to play in the water. I was drawn to it, but I was afraid to go deep in it. I would not get on boats because I did not know how to swim. I missed out on the opportunities to explore the lakes and be out on the water because of fear.

I went to stay with my brother's grandparents one summer and that was where I was forced to face my fear. My older brother was taking swimming lessons at the time.

Like I said, I loved water but was deafly afraid of it. My brother's grandparents said they would pay for me to take swimming lessons. I was excited but scared stiff. I saw the pool that looked like an ocean to me. I refused to get into the pool. They did not have a lot of money and it was a sacrifice for them to pay for my swimming lessons. They paid for all the lessons up front. I remember my grandfather saying, "If you don't get in that water, I am going to throw you in." I thought he was kidding with all those people around and he was just trying to scare me. What he did not realize is that my fear of water was greater than my respect for him at the time. I got into the water up to my waist out of respect. This went on for the first few lessons. The instructor said, "To learn how to swim, you have to go into the deep." I said okay but was afraid to release control and venture into the deep.

On the third or maybe fourth lesson, the instructor said everyone needed to jump into the deep end of the pool, so they can practice what they have learned in the shallow. I refused. I saw myself losing control and drowning. The water was so deep that I did not think I could manage it or take dominion over it. I stood on the sidelines and watched everyone jump into the deep and survive. I saw little babies, toddlers and old people get into the deep and survive. Then it happened: one kid jumped in with his mouth opened and took in too much water. He started flailing about and the instructor jumped in to save him. The instructor said, "You panicked and that is why you almost drowned. Never panic. Close your mouth when you jump in and remember your training. Your muscles know what to do if you let them. Do not panic and everything will be okay."

When I saw that, I said to myself, "I am not getting in there. It is never going to happen. I am not doing it."

After the commotion died down, the instructor said, "Okay, everyone, back into the deep." I stood there paralyzed, then I walked over to the shallow part of the pool and sat in a chair. My older brother tried to dare me into the deep. My mom tried to bribe me; nothing worked because I was too scared. Then my grandfather came over to me and said, "You will face your fear. Come with me." I got up and walked with him. He showed me the deep and said, "You can swim." Then he picked me up and threw me in. You know what, he was right, I could swim, and I did that day. I was held captive by an illusion. My fear had me chained down to what could happen. When I got into the deep, I was mad, but in a few moments my muscles and training took over after I got over the initial shock of being thrown into the deep without my permission.

I calmed myself and swam. I love water and swimming to this day. I have taught my children's friends and anyone who would let me teach them how to swim. Most urban black children do not know how to swim and are afraid of water. There were not many opportunities to swim in the inner city. I respect my grandfather for tossing me into the deep end of the pool. If he did not do that, I would have never realized how much I love water and swimming. It is so beautiful to face your fear and know that it was all a nightmare of your own making. Get the training but at some point, you are going to have to go to the deep end of the pool, if you want to do what is necessary to swim.

Being thrown into the deep end of the pool taught me that what I feared was miniscule and mostly in my head. I could swim, I was just afraid to test myself because I lacked self-confidence. Fear will keep you from doing what you know you can do, going where you should go and being the person that you are supposed to be. Fear will change you into a monster of sorts; it will disfigure you from the inside out. Your world view will become distorted and you will remain a card-carrying member of the "walking dead," afraid to move. That was me: I was afraid that I would drown, despite all the lifeguards and instructors being there with me in the event that I should panic and begin to drown. Fear held me captive, until a force greater than my feet threw me into the deep end of the pool. God is such a force for all of us. He wants us to face our fears with faith and a surety that He is right there with us, never leaving us. There are no F-bomb lessons here; I think the lesson was in my story about facing my fears.

Chapter 5
Trusting The Love Of Christ For Us In The Face Of Our Crisis

When written in Chinese, the word "crisis" is composed of two characters: one represents danger and the other represents opportunity.[7]

Jesus Christ is the greatest Lifeguard on duty. Jesus was a great example of a lifeguard in that He gave His life to guard ours from eternal damnation. We deserve to die as we are all sinners and have broken the law of God. We could not save ourselves, so in steps Jesus, the Lifeguard of all lifeguards. He jumped into the deep end of the pool and tells us to trust Him, look at Him, rest in Him and He will take us where we need to go. He will bring us up from the depths of darkness and place us on the shore of right fellowship. This recovery mission places us into the family as sons and daughters of God, the Father.

---

[7]John F. Kennedy

Along with saving our souls from eternal damnation, Jesus offered us hope in place of our fears, in place of our "what ifs." "What if...?" is where the seed of fear starts for most of us. We ask that question from the negative side of the equation and rarely from the positive side. We say things to ourselves and the world, "What if I fail? What if I am not good enough? What if this is not for me? What if...?" Consider this, "What if you are good enough? What if you are in the right place at the right time and this is your test to prove just that? What if you said, 'I can do all things through Christ who strengthens me?' What if God called you for such a time as this; to take you from the shallows to the deep ocean of faith to provide for you, so you will see that He has been guarding your life before you were even born?"

Consider this for a moment: Christ came that we may have life and have it more abundantly. To have an abundance of anything means there is an abundance of that thing. Think about it like this: fear robs you of abundance by telling you that there is lack, scarcity and not enough to go around. This is the great lie: there is not enough. When we hear that there is not enough, what we really hear is there is not enough for me to get what I need, want, or desire. When we take that lie and internalize it like we do, it becomes a WMD (Weapon of Mass Destruction) in our lives and that is a fear bomb being set and detonated.

Here is the truth of the matter: there is more than enough to go around. When God placed us in our mother's womb, we brought with us all that we needed to do what He sent us to do. We came stocked with all the strength, power, grace, and faith we require to do life on earth. Last time I checked, God did not pack fear in the knapsack, backpack, or the cooler of our souls. Instead, He packed love, power, and a sound mind. Where did we get fear from, since it did not come here with us? We got fear from the world. The world deals in fear like a commodity traded for false security. They sell fear to control, manipulate and steal from the people, all in the name of their father, the devil, the father of lies. This is where fear came from: the author of lies, the devil. He tells you as soon as he has your attention that you are not enough. He plants the seeds of doubt and then walks away knowing that if you are not aware of who you are, you will let that seed grow in the garden of your mind unchecked. His job is done; you have just been tainted with the spirit of fear and you do not even know you picked it up.

Now here is where it becomes criminal and has reached crisis proportion; he has been doing this for thousands of years. He has agents of fear working for him, good meaning parents, teachers, friends, and relatives telling you what they see; not what God said, but what they see. What do they see: lack, evil and the world going to hell in a handbasket already set ablaze. This can be the farthest from the truth. If we look for that, we will see those issues, but if we turn our focus from the world to Him, the Lover and Creator of our souls, we will see that it is just another illusion cooked up by fear. For us to disarm the fear bombs in our lives, we must first recognize them for what they are. They have kept us distracted from the truth: who God says we are and why we are here; His opinion is the only opinion that matters. If God said it, then we are that and what we see is not the whole truth, but a piece or a fragment of truth. If we want to know the truth, we must seek to hear our Father in heaven. His voice is the only voice that can tell us who we are in truth.

A little caution often helps you to recognize when you are about to do something dangerous and it could help you to make a safer choice. Playing it safe is not a life of faith, but of mere existence. We live to get along instead of getting to the mountain top of our purpose and destiny.

You might find yourself fearful of things that are not dangerous, for example, public speaking. If you really want to go on a vacation to Europe, but your fear of flying prevents you from setting foot on an airplane, you might feel like your fear prevents you from living your dream. These are the F-bombs and the anxiety land mines of life. They are self-inflicted traumatic chaos that we feed on for false sustainability. We hold to these lies as if they could ever save us, protect us, and elevate us to our true self. They cannot and never will lift us up; they will only hold us where we are. Living an abundant life is likened to being a shark in the ocean; we cannot go in reverse and as soon as we stop moving forward, we die. If we want more out of life, we must move forward, leaving the destruction of fear in our wake.

What does the fear bomb look like? How can you quickly recognize a fear bomb being detonated in your life? The answer is simple, but the explanation is a tad bit more complicated. Here is the reason: sometimes, or most times, we think the fear bomb is us being cautious, which is a good thing. We rarely see that we are walking in fear and have come to a fork in the road between life and death and we have chosen death. Consider the pros and cons of not facing your fear. If you decide to proceed, the best way to conquer a fear is to face your fears head-on.

A fear of tsunamis is not a big deal, if you live one thousand miles away from the ocean. However, it may be a problem if you live on the coast and you panic every time you hear about earthquakes, storms, or high tides because you think you might be in danger. Have an internal conversation with yourself about what your fears are stopping you from doing and consider if it is a problem that you need to confront. Are your fears causing you to lead a less fulfilling life than the one you hoped for?

THE F--- BOMB

We can choose not to move, live, and speak in faith. This is death. If we are not moving forward in faith, we are dying on our feet. Life produces more life; life feeds on life and death feeds on death. When you are afraid to move in any direction that can benefit you and others, you are the "standing dead." You are dead and quickly dying. Fear keeps you focused on the little you have, instead of the much God promised to provide. Fear bombs are always selfish, self-centered, and self-absorbing. You know you are in fear when all your thoughts are about you not being _____, (fill in the blank).

Who do you trust? Will you believe the Creator of the world or the father of lies? It is your choice; you can stop those F-Bombs from going off in your life and the lives of others by doing three things: have faith, walk in faith, and speak faith-filled words. Faith is light, and fear is darkness. When you shine light on darkness, the darkness disappears; this applies to your faith as well. When you operate in faith, your fear must disappear. Please do not forget that fear has taken root in most of our lives and the lives of our family and friends. We may have to distance ourselves from the "fear contaminated," until we are strong enough in our faith in God to withstand the fiery darts of fear that they will so subtly throw our way. This does not mean we disown them; it simply means we take care to guard our hearts. We must be purposeful about calling faith into our lives and starving fear to death. When someone says, "Man, the world is bad," do not agree with them. Instead, say, "I think it is better than it was and, if we do our part, it will get better." This is quickly recognizing and taking the seed of fear out of the equation.

F-bombs are lurking behind every word, corner thought and unchecked emotion. Fear is real to the fearful, but fear is an illusion to the faith-filled. Do you plan to live in fear or faith? Whatever you choose, you will get just that, so choose wisely. Often, we want to be in control, so we do nothing because of fear. To be in control, give your fear to the Lord and walk in the truth that God cares for you and has not given, nor will He ever give you, the spirit of fear. Fear is from the inner me, that is, the enemy of your future. The devil is often within you, not outside of you.

Do not let your interior fear destroy the future you. If you are afraid to step out on what God gave you, how can you trust that He will provide for you? You cannot. Faith and fear are both like muscles and the more you use one, the stronger it becomes. Do not let your words build a WMD (Weapon of Mass Destruction) in your inner world, that will eventually blow up your outer world. We say some "dumb stuff" about ourselves out of fear, then we want God to come in and bless the mess we have made. Why should He bless it, when He gave us power over fear through our tongue? We often say what we feel and not what God told us. Fear will kill and destroy you, if you operate in it.

Lesson 7 - Life Happens, But Do Not Expect The Worse

Bad things do happen in life, but they may not happen to you. Use your imagination to allow feelings to drift by like a cloud in the sky or a leaf on a stream. That moment of emotional distance from your feelings can result in a more peaceful, productive, problem-solving state of mind.

Lesson 8 - Develop An Attitude Of Thankfulness

The more time and energy you devote to fearful or negative thoughts, the more power you give them. The effect can be stifling to your desired positive behaviors. If you feel negative and the push to act in that negativity, do the opposite of those negative thoughts and behaviors. Look at those fears as just that: a stumbling block to your faithful future. Faith is life and fear is death, so choose life.

Lesson 9 - Live Well By Understanding The Risk

The world is not perfectly safe, and intelligent precautions are a part of living a good life. Living life with safety in mind is not the same as living in a state of fear.

So, find solid ground. Enjoy life, feel close to those you love, recognize that fear can make things bigger than they are and accept that we are not able to control what happens. Know that we can and should control how we respond to what happens; we can choose faith or fear. The choice is always ours.

Chapter 6
Know You Can, Even When The World Says You Can't

The secret to living a life of excellence is merely a matter of thinking thoughts of excellence. Really, it is a matter of programming our minds with the kind of information that will set us free.[8]

Earlier this year, the Journal of Science published a study conducted by researchers from the École Polytechnique Fédérale de Lausanne (EPFL) using mice that showed how the brain must re-experience a fear to extinguish it. Initially, the mice froze, but with repeated exposure to the box, and no additional shocks, they eventually relaxed.

We live and die by faith. We live in faith when we move forward in the face of obstacles and fear. We die when we stop moving forward and let our fear reign in our hearts and minds.

---

[8]Charles R. Swindoll

THE F--- BOMB

Many people say, "I guess I don't have that kind of faith. This scares me to death, and I can't move beyond it." I would have to disagree. We all go to restaurants, eat food from people we do not know, in places we have no control over. I would call that faith. We are trusting that they will not harm us. We buy food from the grocery store, with no real idea of where it came from; that is faith. Now fear comes in when we hear of someone at one of these places doing something unethical but, until then, we go there in good faith.

My question is, why not put that same trust and faith in God? Has He not proven to be faithful? Has He ever done anything unethical or left us in any way? Still so many persons have issues trusting Him. Why? Because of the F-bombs that have been set through religious people. Religion is, and has always, operated in "fear marketing." Get saved or go to hell and burn in hell for eternity. That is fear marketing at its best. Follow this religion or have God mad at you: fear marketing.

Jesus said that with love and kindness He has drawn us. In love, there is no fear. In kindness, there is no fear. There is no fear in the spirit that God gave you. Fear is like a bad cold that spreads from one person to another. Your environment and the people you hang around affect how you get F-bombs going off in and around your world. Fear comes from doubt, guilt, and past missteps. When you do something and the results are not what you want, you feel a bit afraid to do that thing again. If you continue on that train of being afraid, it will eventually turn to fear, then that fear will stop you every time from ever doing that thing; it will also keep you from doing new things. You have just been frozen again by fear. Remember the story of the Elephants in the circus? Do not let that fear rope hold you captive any longer. Take authority and escape your fears by facing them.

Fearlessness is not only possible; it is the ultimate joy. When you overcome fear, you are free.[9]

Do not let fear-filled people speak fear-laced words into your faith-built life. Yes, your life was built by faith. Jesus died on the cross in faith knowing that you could, and some would, reject Him. He went to the cross in faith trusting that God, the Father, was going to raise Him from the dead and place Him back in His position. If He did not die in faith, it would make it impossible for us to live by faith. Without faith, it is impossible to please God, and without faith, we cannot live a just life. The Scriptures are clear that the just will live by faith (See Habakkuk 2:4).

---

[9]Thich Nhat Hanh

THE F--- BOMB

If you are not living by faith, you are not just; you are saved but not just. We are saved by grace, but to live a just life, we must have faith.

Again, what are you fearing that has you speaking death into your life, instead of life into your death? What is causing you to think that you are unworthy, when God was clear that you are worthy? Who told you that you are not able to do exceedingly, abundantly above all that you could ask or think in Christ Jesus? Who said that Jesus' blood was not enough to cover a multitude of sins? Who told you that He does not love you, even though He died to show you? Who said that being fearful was keeping it real because you were just speaking what you saw, when Jesus told you to call those thing that were not as though they were, meaning, calling it what you wanted it to be? Who said that you need to fear, when God said He did not give you the spirit of fear, but of love, power, and a sound mind? Why are you living in fear and letting F-bombs explode all around you? This is because you choose to. You are fearful because you choose to listen to the inner you/enemy of faith: fear.

Stop, look, and listen to the promises of Jesus. Keep your eyes on Him and you will destroy every seed of fear in your life and disarm every F-bomb that has been placed in your midst. You are the only one who can stop these F-bombs from exploding in your life. My question to you is: will you?

> You are not here merely to make a living. You are here to enable the world to live more amply, with greater vision, with a finer spirit of hope and achievement. You are here to enrich the world, and you impoverish yourself if you forget the errand.
>
> ~ Woodrow Wilson

If people did not feel fear, they could not protect themselves from legitimate threats, which, in the ancestral world, frequently resulted in life or death consequences.

In the modern world, individuals often fear situations where the stakes are much lower, but their body and brain may still treat the threat as lethal. As a result, people may find themselves avoiding challenges that could benefit them in the long run or hanging back during social interactions for no good reason.

When people today do face deadly or extreme danger, it can sometimes cause lingering trauma.

THE F--- BOMB

How To Move Past Fear

In the past, our human ancestors feared immediate danger, from volcano eruptions to hungry predators. This hyper-focus on image may only be exacerbated by the rise of the internet and social media culture.

Managing fears in today's world can be confusing when they do not necessarily correlate with a clear or obvious danger. A qualified life coach can help a person find ways to let go of fears, develop coping mechanisms, and look for the positive in fear-inducing situations. I am such a Life Coach. It is normal to feel fear, but fear should not stop you from living your best life. Yes, fear can be debilitating to folks that suffer from fear-induced penalization. You are trapped by fear, when the fear is so strong that you cannot seem to move.

Neuroscientists Antonio Damasio and Joseph LeDoux (2012) both point out that people, even researchers, use the terms "emotions" and "feelings" interchangeably.

<u>Emotions</u> and <u>feelings</u> describe two different processes that philosopher William James highlighted: bodily driven ones (emotions) and think-driven ones (feelings).

Understand that fear is an emotion. Emotions are your brain's split-second responses to a situation, and they kick off changes in your body. Damasio explains that some of these bodily changes are perceptible to other people — like shifts in skin coloration (blushing), posture, and facial expression. Other changes, for example, a boom-boom-booming heart, are "perceptible only to the owner of the body in which they take place."

Say you are in a parking garage and there is a slight movement in the shadows; that circuitry in your brain kicks in and sets off neurochemical reactions that put your body on the alert and ready to run or serve up some "whoop-ass." It is only then—after your body gets into the act—that feelings finally come in. Then, in your conscious mind, another feeling may surface about what the situation could mean for you, "Oh my God, it's probably a serial killer, and he'll come beat me with a tire iron, and I'll die a horrible death!"

As Damasio explains, "Emotions play out in the theater of the body; feelings play out in the theater of the mind."

Feelings are your mind's conscious interpretation of the environmental input affecting your body or, as Damasio puts it, feelings are "mental experiences of bodily states."

However, feelings are not just reactions to environmental input. GOOD NEWS: "Your Fears Are Not The Boss of You." You can override fear by facing it. You will feel fear as you move closer to it. Once you move pass it, you will realize that the fear was more mental than physical. Do not let your lack of mental training keep you in bondage. Our caveman mind did not have the luxury to analyze a feeling; it had to react to potential fear and act quickly or that was the end. Most of us do not live in such a time where we must react all the time without thinking about what we are feeling and thinking so we can respond appropriately.

You may have a feeling—like the urge to dodge some scary, ego-filleting challenge—but that does not mean you have to respond: Yes, your lordship! Sure, feelings are motivational tools, but they are not necessarily motivating you in the right direction right now. Your feelings have you looking frantically for someone portly to hide behind.

Your feelings are trying to act in your best interest by protecting you from rejection. "Died of embarrassment," is a figure of speech, not something they write on the coroner's forms.

The fear keeping you from going after what you want has a co-conspirator—your automatic behavior, such as your habits. Because neurons that fire together wire together, creating behavioral grooves, all your ducking instead of doing has turned ducking into your thing. The more you do a behavior in the face of fear, the easier that habit will become your response whenever fear shows up.

Our fears are often overblown and seriously irrational. Psychologist Albert Ellis, the late cofounder of cognitive behavioral therapy, advocated using reason to reappraise our fears—to help us see how absurd many of them actually are. Ellis was influenced by the Stoic philosopher Epictetus, who said that "it is not things or events that disturb us, but the views we take of them"—meaning, it is not what happens or could happen that makes us feel so bad. The ridiculously irrational interpretation is: "I am a rotten, worthless, accidentally employed person who is only still working here because I'm too insignificant for anyone to remember to fire me." It is not the events themselves that drive us into our feelings cave, but our frame that holds the picture of how we view and interpret what just happened.

Use Your Words

You can talk your feelings smaller. We typically see our feelings as abstract mental states but that is a rather dignified view, and dignity is power. Using language requires you to put your mental weight on your brain's higher reasoning department, the prefrontal cortex. With all that increased activity up there in the front office, there is less action in your brain's alarm center; the amygdala, which likely means less anxiety coursing through you.

THE F--- BOMB

When you are facing a challenge, writing down what is worrying you may help you jump off the negative-thinking merry-go-round. Psychologist Sian Beilock[10] found that students who wrote about their worries for about ten minutes beforehand were less anxious and performed about fifteen percent better than those who sat staring into space and hoping for a miracle.

Beilock explains that the mental processing that goes on while writing may allow a person to tame distracting emotions—shrinking anxiety so it no longer takes over so much of what is called working memory. Working memory is kind of like a mental whiteboard—a temporary workspace for information you need to keep accessible—like partial results to a math problem or the ingredients you have already added when you are baking a cake.

It is likewise very helpful to write about painful experiences. The psychologist James Pennebaker's[11] first study on expressive writing saw students doing fifteen minutes of writing for four days in a row about the emotional impact of a traumatic experience. In the month after the study, those who had written down their

---

[10] Science 14 Jan 2011: Vol. 331, Issue 6014, pp. 211-213 DOI: 10.1126/science.1199427

[11] The 1997 Psychological Science paper "Writing About Emotional Experiences as a Therapeutic Process"

experience (along with the emotions that went with it) showed a fifty percent decline in visits to the university's health center.

Pennebaker explains that the benefit of expressive writing seems to come from reinterpreting and making sense of what happened. Good news for those pressed for time: Research by social Psychologist Chad Burton and personality Psychologist Laura King[12] found that just two minutes of daily expressive writing for two consecutive days may do the job to ease your emotional load. Experiments by happiness researcher Sonja Lyubomirsky[13], among others, found that the benefits of recording your feelings for fifteen minutes are comparable to those of writing them down.

Lyubomirsky points out that perhaps because both writing and recording our thoughts involve an "external source"—either on a piece of paper or an electronic device—they

---

[12] Journal of Research in Personality 38(2):150-163 · April 2004 with 2,999 Reads DOI: 10.1016/S0092-6566(03)00058-8

[13] The Costs and Benefits of Writing, Talking, and Thinking About Life's Triumphs and Defeats Sonja Lyubomirsky, Lorie Sousa, and Rene Dickerhoof University of California, Riverside Journal of Personality and Social Psychology Copyright 2006 by the American Psychological Association 2006, Vol. 90, No. 4, 692–708 0022-3514/06/$12.00 DOI: 10.1037/0022-3514.90.4.692

tend to involve a level of organizing, integrating, and analyzing that mere thinking does not.

Now that you have some tools and science to help, will you stop letting the F-bombs explode in your life? The goal of this book was to arm you with tools for success. You have been locked and loaded with the tools to smack fear in the face and win the war on anxiety, so what are you going to do with your new found power?

FEAR is not real but the EMOTIONS and FEELING it produces are. So, tame your FEAR and let your inner conquer your outer, and you will live a greater fulfilled life.

You should be proud of yourself; you have come to the end of this book. I am proud and honored that you shared your time with me. I hope that it was worth it. You have just disarmed all the F-bombs and started the process to unearth all the anxiety land mines that would do you harm. Now you must go and do what you have been afraid to do. Fear is more dangerous than anything you could ever fear. Fear is a mental fantasy of the false events appearing real. It is a head trip, a heart slip and faithless action in mental acrobatics. You are walking into a dark hole on purpose, knowing that in fear there is no escape, except to face that fear head on in faith.

Now go, face your fear head-on in Christ Jesus, knowing that you are only as good as you believe yourself to be. God called you good. God instructed us to say we are strong when we feel weak. I believe when fear is staring us in the face and weighing heavy on our hearts and minds, we can safely say that we are bold; "We got this" in Christ Jesus. Alone we can do nothing. Christ is the limit, not fear, not anxiety and not people. God is the limit and if He says we are good, then we must believe Him. Before you go, I would like to pray for you.

Prayer

Lord, bless this reader. Father, let them come to know You in such a way that no matter what comes their way, they will trust You to get them through it. Humble them, Lord, so they will submit to Your will by faith and resist those fear bombs that will go off in their lives. Let the love of Jesus fill them and show them that You are greater than anything they can ever face. Give them peace, courage, and strength to do what You created them to do in this world. Fear, you have been warned, prepare to be knocked down, knocked out and ultimately destroyed. You will not have any rule, power, or control over this person any longer; they are free from your hold. They have been blood washed in the blood of Jesus Christ; they surrender to His rule and resist yours. Father, I know I am a sinner and that I cannot be all You want me to be, without first surrendering my life to You. Lord, I confess with my mouth that You are

THE F--- BOMB

God and that Jesus is Your Son, whom You sent to die for my sins. Jesus, I accept You as my Lord and Savior. Come into my heart and mind and fill me with Your Holy Spirit; the Comforter You left me. I repent for walking in fear and not by faith. Today, and every day forward, help me to walk by faith, in Jesus name I pray.

Lord, forgive us for doubting Your Word; Your promise to finish the good work You started in us. Forgive us for being fearful of doing what You placed us on the planet to do, which was to be our best in Christ Jesus. Lord, we surrender all our fears to You, in the name of Your Son, Jesus Christ. Amen.

> Beginning today, treat everyone you meet as if they were going to be dead by midnight. Extend to them all the care, kindness and understanding you can muster, and do it with no thought of any reward. Your life will never be the same again.
>
> ~ Og Mandino

GO BE FEARLESS!

YOU CAN DO IT.

www.ingramcontent.com/pod-product-compliance
Lightning Source LLC
Chambersburg PA
CBHW052119110526
44592CB00013B/1671